# THE TURMERIC COOKBOOK

An Hachette UK Company
www.hachette.co.uk

First published in Great Britain in 2017 by Aster, a division of
Octopus Publishing Group Ltd, Carmelite House,
50 Victoria Embankment, London EC4Y 0DZ
www.octopusbooks.co.uk



ISBN 978-1-91202-308-0

A CIP catalogue record for this book is available from the British Library.

Printed and bound in China.

10 9 8 7 6 5 4 3 2 1

**Consultant Publisher** Kate Adams
**Recipe Developer and Food Stylist** Nicole Pisani, Food for Happiness
**Additional Recipes** Oliver Pagani
**Cocktail Recipes** Gosia Zielony
**Senior Designer** Jaz Bahra
**Senior Editor** Leanne Bryan
**Copy Editor** Clare Sayer
**Photographer** Issy Croker
**Props Stylist** Emily Ezekiel
**Production Manager** Caroline Alberti

Page 7 picture credit: Wellcome Library, London

# THE TURMERIC COOKBOOK

Discover the health benefits and uses of turmeric, with 50 delicious recipes

## CONTENTS

INTRODUCTION 6
BREAKFASTS 12
SNACKS & CONDIMENTS 26
SOUPS 40
VEGETARIAN DISHES 54
FISH & MEAT DISHES 74
SWEETS 94
DRINKS 108
BEAUTY 120
INDEX 126

# INTRODUCTION

Turmeric, the spice best known as an ingredient in curries, is one of nature's most powerful ancient healers and has been used medicinally for over 4,500 years. It comes from the root of *Curcuma longa*, a green plant in the ginger family and is grown throughout the tropics, especially in India and Indonesia. On the island of Bali, turmeric is at the heart of their traditional medicine and 'Jamu' tonics are widely available to cure your ailments and boost your well-being.

Turmeric appears in some of the earliest known records of plant medicines. It is mentioned in Egyptian texts and is thought to have been cultivated in the Gardens of Babylon, one of the Seven Wonders of the Ancient World. In India, turmeric plays an important part in Ayurvedic medicine, originating around 2,500 years ago. Inhaling the fumes from burning turmeric was said to alleviate congestion; turmeric paste or juice was used to heal wounds and bruises; and the spice was also used for digestive issues.

Modern medicine is now beginning to confirm many of the reported health benefits of turmeric and especially its anti-cancer properties. Much of the research is focused on one of the main components of turmeric, a substance called curcumin. However, attention is now also being directed at studying the effects of the whole root and the pages that follow will explore all the potential health benefits of this wonder root.

## COOKING WITH TURMERIC

So, we are all starting to hear more about turmeric and how it might be a good idea to include plenty of it in our diets. But beyond curry, how do we do that?

As it happens, alongside the increased attention of the medical community, chefs and healthy foodies have been trying out turmeric in an amazing array of different types of dishes. Traditional 'golden milks' and tonics are growing in popularity; turmeric teas and turmeric honey are now available; and supermarkets are beginning to sell the fresh root alongside ginger, as well as in its ground or powdered form.

Turmeric has a very individual taste that is difficult to describe, except to say it is quite pungent and bitter. However, when combined with other flavours its culinary use widens considerably; for example it goes well with honey and so can be used in desserts, on top of porridge or in granola. You can use it in baking, roasting vegetables, in salad dressings or even in ice cream.

And as turmeric has anti-ageing properties, it can also be used as a natural beauty ingredient, so we've included some different face masks to try and a homemade turmeric soap.

> 'Each spice has a special day to it. For turmeric it is Sunday, when light drips fat and butter-coloured into the bins to be soaked up glowing, when you pray to the nine planets for love and luck.'
>
> — Chitra Banerjee Divakaruni, *The Mistress of Spices*

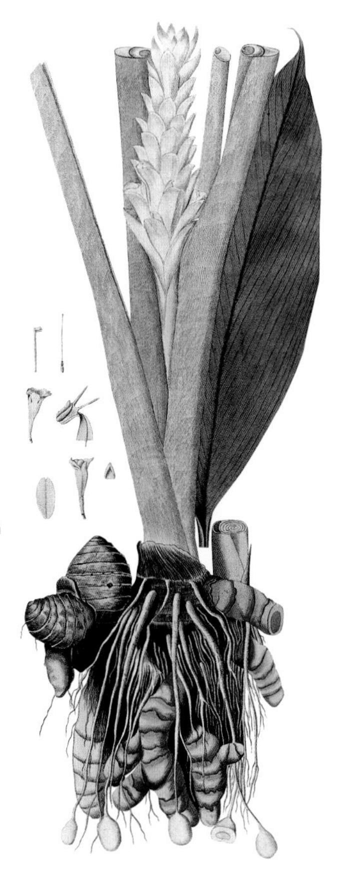

## ANCIENT HEALER, MODERN MEDICINE

While the Assyrians and the Ancient Greeks knew about and used turmeric, it is Asian herbalists – likely due to turmeric needing tropical conditions to thrive – who made the most medicinal use of this spice until the Europeans began to catch up in the late 20th century.

In Ayurveda, the Indian system of herbal medicine, turmeric is thought to 'strengthen and warm' the system. It is used specifically to improve the digestion system and microbiome, to regulate menstruation, relieve the inflammation associated with arthritis and balance the metabolism. It is also used as an anti-inflammatory and antibacterial agent for coughs and colds and on the skin for burns, cuts and bruises.

The ancient Hawaiians are also thought to have used turmeric for conditions including ear and sinus infections, most probably due to the spice's astringent properties. And across Indonesia, the recipes for turmeric tonics are still closely guarded family secrets, used in the traditional herbal healing system known as Jamu, both for general preventative well-being and for the treatment of specific conditions, such as joint pain.

In Europe, serious research on the health properties of turmeric began in Germany in the 1920s, and in the 1960s its benefits to the digestive system started to be discussed. By the 1990s, turmeric was more regularly recommended by western herbalists and today doctors and general practitioners often recommend turmeric as part of a healthy diet, especially for cancer patients.

Research into the heart benefits of turmeric has focused on curcumin, its main active ingredient. This has been shown to have anti-inflammatory effects, and it is also an antioxidant. Inflammation has been linked to heart disease, diabetes, Alzheimer's, stroke and cancer. Antioxidants protect the body from the damage caused by free radicals, which we are exposed to through normal bodily processes such as burning sugars for energy or digestion, and through our environment. The anti-inflammatory and antioxidant effects of turmeric are also linked to benefitting overall health and wellbeing when included in a healthy diet.

Recently, studies have shown the potential anti-cancer benefits of turmeric, specifically when consumed through cooking. It is thought that it may be helpful both as part of a preventative lifestyle and for cancer patients undergoing treatment.

## DOSAGE

It is currently thought that about a teaspoon of fresh or ground turmeric a day is helpful for promoting gut health and general wellness.

## TURMERIC AND BLACK PEPPER

Black pepper contains the compound piperine that helps increase absorption of curcumin. It isn't necessary to always consume turmeric with black pepper, but it has been shown to boost the body's ability to absorb the beneficial properties.

## PREPARATION AND USES

The ground turmeric that we easily recognize from its bright orange colour comes from the fingers that grow from the root. The root is cleaned, boiled and then dried at a low temperature before being processed into a powder. Turmeric can also be used in a similar way to fresh root ginger, grated directly into recipes or infused in oils or in hot water for tea (*see* page 114). Turmeric root is now more readily available in supermarkets and delis – it has a slightly sweeter taste than the powder.

Turmeric can be eaten both raw and cooked. For example you can grate it into dressings, ice cream, or tonics (*see* pages 37, 104 and 111), or add a little to soups and stews (*see* pages 42, 47 and 52).

## WHEN EVERYTHING TURNS YELLOW

The only problem with turmeric is that it can easily discolour your pots and pans, your worktops and even your hands. Lemon juice or white vinegar can remove the colouring, or for more stubborn stains you can use a bleach-based cleaner. If you spill a bit of sauce that has turmeric in it, you can try sprinkling with talcum powder or bicarbonate of soda and then blot gently with kitchen paper. The key is to try not to rub it in! For clothes, sometimes bleach is the only answer, but apparently soaking the item and putting it in sunlight may help to fade the stain. And for your skin, try mixing sugar and water and gently scrubbing your hands; this works as a natural exfoliator at the same time as removing that lovely yellow hue.

# BREAKFASTS

SERVES 2

◇◇◇◇◇◇

# BIRCHER MUESLI
## WITH TURMERIC HONEY

Soaking oats overnight makes breakfast quick and easy in the morning. You can then simply heat them up with a little extra milk or water and serve with a spoonful of turmeric honey, or turn into a Bircher muesli with some chopped fruit and nuts.

---

100g porridge oats
1 tablespoon flaxseeds
1 tablespoon chia seeds
¼ teaspoon ground cinnamon
100ml unsweetened almond milk
200ml water
few drops of vanilla extract
2 apples
juice of ½ lime
2 tablespoons natural yogurt
1 tablespoon hazelnuts, roughly chopped
2 tablespoons turmeric honey (*see* below)
1 teaspoon coconut oil (optional)

**To serve (optional)**
Spiced and Roasted Seeds (*see* page 30)
Thai basil leaves

**For the turmeric honey (makes 200g)**
50g coconut oil
150g raw clear honey
2 teaspoons ground turmeric
¼ teaspoon ground black pepper

First make the turmeric honey. Heat the coconut oil so that it is in liquid form. Add to a bowl with the honey, turmeric and pepper and combine thoroughly. Transfer to a glass jar and store at room temperature until needed.

The night before, mix together the oats, seeds, cinnamon, almond milk, water and vanilla extract in a large bowl and chill in the refrigerator overnight.

In the morning, grate 1 of the apples and stir into the oats with the lime juice, yogurt, chopped hazelnuts and turmeric honey.

Slice the remaining apple and, if liked, sauté in the coconut oil. Use to top the Bircher muesli and finish with a sprinkling of spiced and roasted seeds and a few Thai basil leaves (if using).

MAKES ABOUT 500G

◇◇◇◇◇◇

# COCONUT AND CASHEW GRANOLA

Making your own granola means you can put in all your favourite things. The coconut flakes and cashew nuts here create a light granola while the honey and cinnamon add just the right amount of sweetness.

---

250g jumbo oats
125g raw cashew nuts, roughly chopped
50g pumpkin seeds
50g sunflower seeds
25g golden flaxseeds
½ teaspoon ground cinnamon
½ teaspoon ground turmeric
½ teaspoon ground ginger
2 heaped tablespoons coconut oil
60g raw clear honey
1 teaspoon vanilla extract

Preheat the oven to 140°C (275°F), Gas Mark 1 and line a large baking tray with baking paper.

Mix all the dry ingredients together in a large bowl.

Heat the coconut oil and honey in a saucepan until dissolved, then add the vanilla extract. Pour this into the dry ingredients and stir thoroughly so that all the oats, nuts and seeds are evenly coated.

Pour the granola on to the paper and spread out evenly. Bake for about 1 hour until golden and just crunchy. Allow to cool in the switched-off oven and then gently bring up the sides of the paper to transfer the granola to an airtight jar.

**SERVES 2**

◇◇◇◇◇◇

# DEVILLED SCRAMBLED EGGS
## WITH AVOCADO ON TOAST

Adding a few spices to your eggs makes the perfect accompaniment to avocado on toast for a great Sunday brunch.

---

- 4 eggs
- ½ teaspoon ground turmeric
- ¼ teaspoon hot paprika
- ¼ teaspoon chilli powder
- 6 tablespoons milk (or non-dairy alternative)
- 2 thick slices of sourdough bread
- extra virgin olive oil, for drizzling
- 1 ripe avocado
- juice of ½ lemon
- 2 teaspoons butter or coconut oil
- good pinch of chilli flakes
- sea salt flakes

Crack the eggs into bowl and whisk with the spices and milk.

Preheat the grill. Drizzle the sourdough slices with extra virgin olive oil, sprinkle with sea salt flakes and put under the grill.

Meanwhile, cut the avocado in half and remove the stone. Spoon it out and mash with the lemon juice and a little salt.

Melt the butter or coconut oil in a nonstick frying pan over a high heat and add the eggs and a good pinch of salt. Leave for several seconds to start cooking on the bottom and then gently fold the eggs over and into one another – do not stir. Remove from the heat when it is still just slightly liquid.

Spread the toasted sourdough with the mashed avocado and spoon over the scrambled eggs. Sprinkle with the chilli flakes and serve immediately.

SERVES 2

◇◇◇◇◇◇

# FRITTATA

The best way to get anyone to eat more greens is to find a way to combine them with eggs and cheese. This frittata is simple but the trick is to get the heat high enough for the eggs to puff up when they hit the pan, similar to an omelette.

---

- 1 tablespoon coconut oil
- 1 teaspoon grated fresh root ginger
- 1 teaspoon grated fresh turmeric
- 200g cavolo nero, stalks removed and leaves roughly chopped
- 4 large eggs
- knob of butter
- 1 tablespoon crème fraîche
- 100g ewes' cheese, shaved
- sea salt and ground black pepper

Preheat the oven to 220°C (425°F), Gas Mark 7.

Heat the coconut oil in a small, nonstick, ovenproof frying pan. Add the ginger and turmeric and fry over a medium heat until you can smell the aroma. Add the cavolo nero, season with salt and pepper and allow to wilt. Remove from the heat, transfer to a bowl and massage the wilted leaves with your hands.

Whisk the eggs vigorously while you melt the butter in the same pan over a high heat. Stir the crème fraîche into the eggs and once the pan is very hot and the butter is foaming, add the egg and crème fraîche mixture. The edges should puff up straightaway. Add shavings of cheese and the wilted greens before transferring the pan to the oven. Cook for about 5 minutes, until the top is puffed and golden. Serve immediately.

**SERVES 2**

◇◇◇◇◇◇

# SMOKED MACKEREL TURMERIC CONGEE

Congee is simply rice that has been cooked longer that usual so that it goes very soft. It's similar to risotto but comes from Asia and is often eaten for breakfast as a kind of savoury porridge.

---

2 tablespoons sesame oil
25g fresh root ginger, peeled and thinly sliced
3 garlic cloves, thinly sliced
1 teaspoon ground turmeric
200g short-grain rice, washed thoroughly
4 dried shiitake mushrooms, rehydrated in warm water
450ml chicken or fish stock
450ml water
4 tablespoons light soy sauce

**To serve**

2 eggs
1 tablespoon vinegar, for poaching
2 large smoked mackerel fillets, at room temperature
1 shallot, thinly sliced
1 radish, thinly sliced
few sprigs of lemon verbena (or use picked coriander leaves)

Heat 1 tablespoon of the sesame oil in a saucepan over a medium heat and lightly fry the ginger and garlic. You don't want much colour so fry until they're aromatic and just slightly softer. Add the turmeric and stir well.

Add the rice and the shiitake mushrooms to the pan and thoroughly mix everything through. The mushrooms are to add a bit of background umami to the dish.

Add the stock and the water and cook for about 1 hour over a low heat, or until the rice becomes soft and porridge-like in texture with a fair amount of liquid left in the pan. So if the congee gets too dry just add some more water or stock until the consistency has returned. Once the rice is cooked and you have the desired texture, add the soy sauce and the other tablespoon of sesame oil.

Meanwhile, poach the eggs. Bring a saucepan of water to a rolling boil and add the vinegar. Crack the eggs into a ramekin or small cup and gently tip into the water. Poach for 6 minutes and then remove with a slotted spoon and drain on kitchen paper.

Divide the rice between two bowls and top each one with flakes of the mackerel and a poached egg. Garnish with sliced shallot, sliced radish and lemon verbena sprigs.

# SNACKS & CONDIMENTS

**MAKES 10**

◇◇◇◇◇◇

# BLISS BALLS

You can store these balls in the refrigerator for up to 5 days. They are great as a snack for when you fancy a treat or need a burst of energy, and are particularly good for days when you are exercising.

---

70g whole almonds
30g flaxseeds
30g desiccated coconut, plus extra for rolling
120g dried apple, soaked in hot water for 1 minute and then drained
1 teaspoon ground turmeric
½ teaspoon ground cinnamon
1 tablespoon raw cacao powder
2 tablespoons coconut oil, melted
2 tablespoons raw clear honey (or use the Turmeric Honey on page 15 and omit the turmeric above)

Put all the ingredients into a food processor and blend to a paste.

Roll into balls about the size of a walnut and then coat in the extra desiccated coconut.

**MAKES 200G**

◇◇◇◇◇◇

# SPICED AND ROASTED SEEDS

The orange juice adds a sweetness to this savoury snack. The seeds are great for taking in a pot to the office, or you can use them to add a bit of crunch to soups and salads.

---

- 100g pumpkin seeds
- 100g sunflower seeds
- 1 tablespoon olive oil
- juice of 1 lime
- juice of 1 orange
- ½ teaspoon ground turmeric
- ½ teaspoon mild chilli powder
- ½ teaspoon sea salt flakes

Preheat the oven to 180°C (350°F), Gas Mark 4 and line a baking tray with baking paper.

Mix all the ingredients together in a bowl and then spread out over the lined tray. Roast for 30–40 minutes, shaking the seeds halfway through cooking, until golden and crunchy.

Allow to cool and transfer to an airtight jar.

MAKES ABOUT 20 SMALL OATCAKES

# TURMERIC AND BLACK PEPPER OATCAKES

A little turmeric goes a long way, especially when you see the colour of these oatcakes.

---

- 250g porridge oats
- 1 tablespoon olive oil
- ¼ teaspoon ground turmeric
- good pinch of ground black pepper
- ¼ teaspoon sea salt flakes
- flour, for dusting

Preheat the oven to 180°C (350°F), Gas Mark 4 and line a large baking tray with baking paper.

Put the oats into a large bowl. Add the olive oil, turmeric, pepper and sea salt and mix together.

Fill a jug with half boiled, half cool water. Add enough of it to the oats to make them sticky enough to form a ball that binds together. If you add too much water, just add some more oats. Roll out the ball on a lightly floured surface to a large rectangle about 3mm thick. Use a round cutter (about 6–7cm) to cut circles and use a spatula to lift them on to the lined baking tray.

Bake until golden, 20–30 minutes, depending on thickness. Transfer to a wire rack to cool.

MAKES 1 × 400G TUB

# TURMERIC HUMMUS

For a cheat's version of this, simply stir a little ground turmeric and lemon zest into ready-made hummus, although there's something about making your own that can't be beaten.

---

- 400g can chickpeas, rinsed and drained
- zest and juice of 1 lemon
- 1 teaspoon sweet paprika
- 1 teaspoon ground turmeric
- ½ teaspoon mild chilli powder
- 6 tablespoons extra virgin olive oil, plus extra for drizzling
- 2 tablespoons tahini
- 1 teaspoon sea salt flakes
- 2 tablespoons water (or more if needed)

**To serve**

- honey, for drizzling (optional)
- Spiced and Roasted Seeds (*see* page 30)
- a handful of microherbs
- Turmeric and Black Pepper Oatcakes (*see* page 31), (optional)

Put all the ingredients in a food processor and blend until smooth, scraping down the sides of the processor as you go. Add more water if needed to get the right consistency.

Transfer to a bowl and add a drizzle of honey or olive oil. Garnish with a sprinkling of spiced and roasted seeds and a handful of microherbs. Serve with turmeric and black pepper oatcakes, if liked.

MAKES 1 LOAF

# TURMERIC BANANA BREAD

This is a really easy and tasty way to use up overripe bananas. This recipe uses spelt flour but you could just as easily use a gluten-free flour. The coconut oil and bananas help to keep it moist and it's delicious toasted with a little butter.

---

200g spelt flour
2 teaspoons baking powder
½ teaspoon bicarbonate of soda
¾ teaspoon sea salt
1 teaspoon ground ginger
1 teaspoon ground turmeric
50ml coconut oil, melted
50g coconut sugar (or use soft light brown sugar)
1 teaspoon vanilla extract
3–4 ripe bananas, mashed
2 large eggs
butter, to serve

Preheat the oven to 180°C (350°F), Gas Mark 4 and oil or butter a 21 x 11cm loaf tin.

Sift the flour, baking powder, bicarbonate of soda, salt, ginger and turmeric into a bowl. In another bowl combine the melted coconut oil, coconut sugar, vanilla extract, mashed bananas and eggs until quite smooth with a few banana lumps.

Add the wet ingredients to the dry and stir until just combined into an airy batter. Scrape into the loaf tin and bake until a tester skewer comes out clean, about 50–60 minutes.

Allow to cool in the tin for 10 minutes and then run a knife around the edge of the loaf to release; turn out onto a wire rack to cool completely. Cut into slices and serve, toasted if liked, and spread with butter, or transfer to a cake tin and keep for 3–4 days.

MAKES 3 × 200G JARS

◇◇◇◇◇◇

# TURMERIC PICKLES

Pickles add a sharpness and crunch and are great for enjoying with a slice of cheese, cold cuts or on picnics.

---

200g daikon radish, peeled
200g carrots, peeled
200g turnips
5 curry leaves per jar (fresh or dried)
1 red chilli per jar, deseeded and halved lengthways
2 strips of lemon rind per jar

**For the pickling liquor**

1.2 litres warm water
160ml rice wine vinegar
5 tablespoons coconut or granulated sugar
2 tablespoons sea salt
½ teaspoon ground turmeric

Start by sterilizing the pickling jars you are going to use by pouring boiling hot water into them and leaving them for several minutes. Pour the water out and leave them to air dry.

Quarter the daikon radish lengthways so you have 4 long pieces, then cut each quarter into chunky pieces. The carrots can be cut in half lengthways and then cut into chunky half-moons. You can cut the turnips any which way as long as they are roughly the same size as the rest.

Divide them evenly between the jars but don't over pack them. Put the curry leaves, chillies and strips of lemon rind into the jars alongside the vegetables.

For the pickling liquor heat the water and vinegar in a saucepan over a very low heat until it is nearly hot and dissolve the sugar, salt and turmeric into it.

Pour the liquor evenly between the jars so the vegetables are covered. You may need to press the vegetables down slightly. Seal the jars and put in the refrigerator for 3 days to pickle. If you don't have 3 days to spare, you can bring the liquor to boil before pouring it on to the veg, sealing the jar and allowing it to cool down. You don't quite get the flavour but it will still be a decent pickle.

MAKES 200G

◇◇◇◇◇◇

# TURMERIC MUSTARD

When you have a few pickles and condiments on hand, you'll be able to add the benefits of turmeric to your dishes without even thinking about it.

---

- 50g mustard seeds (white or mixed)
- 25g mustard powder
- 2 teaspoons sea salt flakes
- 150ml water
- 3 tablespoons apple cider vinegar
- 1 teaspoon ground turmeric
- 2 tablespoons raw clear honey

Mix together the mustard seeds, mustard powder and sea salt in a bowl and add the water, combining well. Set aside for 10 minutes before adding the apple cider vinegar, turmeric and honey; mix well.

Transfer to an airtight jar and allow to set overnight in the refrigerator. This will keep for up to 6 months in the refrigerator.

MAKES 500ML

◇◇◇◇◇◇

# TURMERIC-INFUSED OIL

When you have this oil on hand in the kitchen you can make quick dressings or simply drizzle it over dishes both to add flavour and to give an immediate health boost.

---

- 250ml avocado oil
- 250ml extra virgin olive oil
- 2 tablespoons grated fresh turmeric (or use 2 heaped tablespoons ground turmeric)
- 1 teaspoon coarsely ground black pepper

Add all the ingredients to a glass bottle, seal and shake. Leave to infuse for 2 weeks before using.

# SOUPS

**SERVES 2**

◇◇◇◇◇◇

# GINGER AND TURMERIC CARROT SOUP

This is a quick and very tasty soup, perfect for a cold winter day.

---

- 1 tablespoon groundnut oil
- ½ onion, chopped
- 1 teaspoon grated fresh root ginger
- 1 teaspoon grated fresh turmeric or ground turmeric
- ⅛ teaspoon ground black pepper, plus extra to season
- 250g carrots, roughly chopped
- 400ml hot vegetable stock
- 40g cashew nuts, roughly chopped
- ½ teaspoon mild chilli powder
- sea salt flakes

Heat the oil in a saucepan over a low–medium heat, add the onion and sauté for about 10 minutes until soft. Add the ginger, turmeric and black pepper and stir through before adding the carrots.

Continue to stir the carrots for another couple of minutes, then add the stock. Bring to the boil, then reduce the heat and simmer for 10–15 minutes, or until the carrots can be easily pierced with a sharp knife.

Transfer the soup to a blender and process until smooth; taste and adjust the seasoning.

Mix the chopped cashew nuts with the mild chilli powder and dry roast in a frying pan for a few minutes over a low heat.

Serve the soup in bowls with the spiced cashew nuts scattered over the top.

**SERVES 2**

◇◇◇◇◇◇

# KITCHARI

This recipe is based on an Ayurvedic cleansing soup; if you are doing the cleanse, you eat only kitchari for a certain number of days. We've included it as it's just a surprisingly delicious recipe.

---

100g green mung beans, rinsed and soaked overnight
1 teaspoon ground turmeric
¼ teaspoon ground black pepper
1 sheet of kombu seaweed or ¼ teaspoon asafoetida
20g butter
¼ teaspoon mustard seeds
¼ teaspoon cumin seeds
¼ teaspoon fennel seeds
¼ teaspoon nigella seeds
6 dried curry leaves
zest and juice of 1 lemon
sea salt flakes

**For the crispy onions (optional)**
1 onion, sliced into rings
plain flour, for dusting
vegetable oil, for frying

**To serve**
natural yogurt
chopped nuts
Spiced and Roasted Seeds (*see* page 30)
pea shoots

Rinse the mung beans a couple of times, drain and put into a saucepan with 1 litre of water.

Add the turmeric, black pepper and seaweed or asafoetida and bring to the boil. Reduce to a low simmer and cook for about an hour, until the beans are soft.

Heat the butter in a frying pan over a medium heat and when bubbling, add the seeds, curry leaves and lemon zest. When the seeds begin to pop, remove from the heat and carefully add to the kitchari. Add the lemon juice and sea salt to taste.

Take the kitchari off the heat, cover and rest for 5–10 minutes while you prepare the crispy onions (if using).

Heat the vegetable oil in a wok over a high heat. Dip the onion rings in flour and then carefully lower into the hot oil with tongs. When they are golden and crispy remove from the pan and drain on kitchen paper.

Top the kitchari with any or all of the serving suggestions: crispy onions, a dollop of natural yogurt, some chopped nuts, spiced and roasted seeds and pea shoots.

SERVES 4

◇◇◇◇◇◇

# SQUASH AND COCONUT DHAL

Dhal is a great standby to have during the week and the added butternut squash here makes it a really fulfilling meal in a bowl. Tamari is not an everyday companion for dhal or turmeric but it adds a lovely flavour here.

---

225g yellow split peas, rinsed and drained
600ml vegetable stock
500g butternut squash, peeled, deseeded and diced
2 tablespoons tamari
50g coconut cream
2 tablespoons olive oil
2 teaspoons mustard seeds
1 onion, thinly sliced
1 teaspoon ground turmeric

Put the split peas into a saucepan with the stock, bring to a simmer and cook gently for about 30 minutes. Add the squash, tamari and coconut cream and cook for another 15–20 minutes until the squash is soft. If you prefer your soup smooth, transfer to a blender and process until smooth.

Heat the olive oil in a small frying pan. Add the mustard seeds and stir until they start popping. Add the onion and soften for 10 minutes over a low–medium heat. Stir in the turmeric and cook for a few more minutes.

Ladle the soup into bowls and top with the aromatic onions. Serve immediately.

SERVES 2

◇◇◇◇◇◇

# BACON AND EGG-DROP MISO

This is a really quick soup, perfect for lunch or after exercising. Make it vegetarian by leaving out the bacon – it's just as good.

---

2 streaky bacon rashers, chopped into small pieces
2 spring onions, thinly sliced
2 teaspoons brown miso paste
½ teaspoon grated fresh turmeric or ground turmeric
2 large handfuls of baby spinach
2 eggs, beaten

Heat a nonstick saucepan and fry the bacon over a medium heat, adding the spring onions after a couple of minutes.

Dissolve the miso paste in a little just-boiled water and add to the pan, along with about 500ml just boiled water and the turmeric. Allow the flavours to infuse for a couple of minutes before adding the spinach.

When the spinach has wilted down a little, slowly add the beaten eggs to the soup, ideally through a slotted spoon to help create ribbons.

As soon as the egg sets, remove from the heat, divide between 2 bowls and serve.

SERVES 4

◇◇◇◇◇◇

# CHICKEN KHAO SOI

This is a very hearty and warming soup. It looks like a lot of ingredients but once you have them, making the curry paste is a case of just blitzing everything together in a blender. The result is an amazing combination of flavours. The paste will keep in the refrigerator for up to 14 days in an airtight container so you can make it in advance and keep it on hand for when you fancy a bowl of noodles and vegetables.

---

2 teaspoons coconut oil
2 x 400ml cans coconut milk
500ml chicken stock
4 chicken thighs or drumsticks
4 tablespoons Thai fish sauce
1 tablespoon sugar
vegetable oil, for frying
200g firm tofu, cubed
cornflour, for dusting
300g soba noodles

**For the curry paste**
4 dried red chillies
3 shallots, quartered
8 garlic cloves
2.5cm piece of galangal, peeled and roughly chopped (or 1 teaspoon galangal paste)
2.5cm piece of fresh root ginger, peeled and roughly chopped
20g fresh coriander, roughly chopped

First make the curry paste. Rehydrate the dried chillies in about 50ml hot water for about 20 minutes until they are soft. Drain, reserving the liquid. Put the chillies into a blender with all the remaining paste ingredients (or a bowl if using a hand-held blender). Add some of the chilli water and blend to a smooth paste.

Heat the coconut oil in a heavy-based saucepan and add the curry paste. Fry the paste over a medium heat, stirring constantly, for about 3–4 minutes until it has browned slightly.

Shake the cans of coconut milk well so it isn't split and add to the pan. Mix together well and then add the chicken stock. Bring to the boil, then reduce the heat and simmer for a further 5 minutes.

Add the chicken thighs or drumsticks to the simmering liquid and cook the chicken for 25–30 minutes until it is soft and tender. Remove and allow to cool for a few minutes, then shred the meat off the bone so you have some chunks and some finely shredded meat; rustic is

1 tablespoon ground coriander
1 tablespoon ground turmeric
1 teaspoon curry powder

**To garnish**
wilted tatsoi
a couple of handfuls of toasted cashews
fresh sprigs of coriander
sliced spring onions
juice of 1 lime

the aim. Add the meat back into the sauce, along with the Thai fish sauce and the sugar.

Meanwhile, heat some vegetable oil in a frying pan or wok over a medium–high heat. Dust the tofu cubes lightly in cornflour and then fry for a few minutes until golden brown on all sides. Remove from the pan and drain on kitchen paper.

Cook the soba noodles according to the packet instructions, then drain. Portion the noodles, chicken and fried tofu into 4 soup bowls, then pour the soup over. Finish each bowl with some wilted tatsoi, a handful of toasted cashews, some sprigs of coriander, sliced spring onion and a squeeze of lime juice.

**SERVES 4**

◇◇◇◇◇◇

# RASAM
## WITH SASHIMI AND WILTING GREENS

There is a bit of theatre in this dish as you pour the rasam broth over the fish and greens at the table. Alternatively, you could poach the salmon in the broth for a few minutes. Passing the rasam through a sieve gives you a clear broth that is filled with flavour.

---

65g tamarind paste
750ml hot water (from a boiled kettle)
1 tomato, quartered
400g good-quality skinless salmon fillet, very thinly sliced at an angle
4 tablespoons Greek yogurt
100g baby spinach
100g baby kale

**For the rasam paste**
½ teaspoon cracked black pepper
1 teaspoon ground turmeric
4 dried red chillies
1 teaspoon cumin seeds
4 garlic cloves
20g coriander stems

**For the temper**
1 teaspoon coconut oil
1 teaspoon black mustard seeds
½ teaspoon cumin seeds
10–12 dried curry leaves
¼ teaspoon asafoetida

First put the tamarind paste and hot water into a large saucepan to steep for about 10 minutes.

Meanwhile, start making the rasam paste by pounding all the ingredients together in a pestle and mortar until they form a coarse paste. Alternatively, you can blitz the ingredients roughly in a blender, but the idea is to keep the paste coarse.

By this time, the tamarind should be soft. Mix the tamarind water with the rasam paste, add the tomato and place over a low–medium heat to start to warm through.

For the temper, heat the coconut oil in a frying pan. Add the mustard seeds and, once they start popping, add the cumin. Allow the cumin to brown slightly (30 seconds or so). Add the curry leaves and asafoetida and stir for several seconds. Add to the broth in the pan, bring to the boil, then reduce the heat and simmer for 5–6 minutes. Take off the heat and strain the rasam, pressing on the tomatoes to get all the flavour.

Now you're ready to serve. Add a tablespoon of yogurt to each bowl. Arrange the spinach and baby kale on top, then place 3 or 4 slices of the salmon on top of the greens. Bring the rasam back to the boil, serve the bowls at the table and pour the piping hot rasam over the fish.

**SERVES 2**

◇◇◇◇◇◇

# COCONUT CHICKEN SOUP
## WITH TURMERIC AND KALE

The sweetness of coconut goes very well with turmeric; here the use of coconut water as opposed to coconut milk creates a light, fresh and healthy soup that warms the body and soul.

---

1 tablespoon coconut oil
1 small onion, chopped
200ml coconut water
200ml hot chicken stock
1 teaspoon grated fresh turmeric or ground turmeric
¼ teaspoon ground black pepper
100g kale, stalks removed and leaves shredded
1 baby gem lettuce, halved
1 tablespoon olive oil
100g leftover roast chicken
squeeze of lemon juice, to taste (optional)
sea salt flakes

Melt half the coconut oil in a heavy-based saucepan and sauté the onion over a medium heat until soft, about 8–10 minutes. Add the coconut water, stock, turmeric and black pepper. Keep at a low simmer.

Heat the remaining coconut oil in a frying pan or wok and sauté the kale with a good pinch of sea salt for a few minutes until softened.

Place a griddle pan over a high heat, brush the baby gem halves with the olive oil and griddle on both sides for 2–3 minutes.

Place the kale, lettuce and chicken into bowls and pour over the hot coconut chicken stock. Taste and add lemon juice if needed. Serve immediately.

# VEGETARIAN DISHES

SERVES 4 AS A SIDE DISH

◇◇◇◇◇◇

# CORN ON THE COB
## WITH TURMERIC BUTTER

This is perfect for a summer barbecue. Adding the spices to the butter gives an extra element of flavour. If you are using fresh corn on the cob, you will need to boil them for about 10 minutes before grilling.

---

- 4 frozen mini corn cobs (or use fresh corn cobettes)
- 80g unsalted butter
- ½ teaspoon grated fresh turmeric or ground turmeric
- ½ teaspoon ground cumin
- sea salt and ground black pepper

Either on a barbecue or in a griddle pan, cook the corn until soft and a little charred.

Melt the butter in a small saucepan and add the turmeric and cumin. Allow the spices to cook a little in the butter for a few minutes for the flavours to infuse.

Serve the corn with the melted butter poured over and season generously with salt and pepper.

SERVES 2

◇◇◇◇◇◇

# NEW POTATO SALAD
## WITH TURMERIC TAHINI DRESSING

Potatoes are given a bit of a twist here, replacing the usual mayo with a vibrant tahini and turmeric dressing.

---

500g new potatoes, washed
leaves from ½ bunch of fresh mint
4 spring onions, thinly sliced on the diagonal
1 teaspoon sumac
sea salt and ground black pepper

**For the dressing**
80ml tahini
juice of 1 lemon
30ml extra virgin olive oil
2 tablespoons water
1 teaspoon ground turmeric

Put the potatoes in a large pan and fill with enough cold water to cover them fully. Add a small handful of salt and 2 sprigs of the mint to the water before covering with a lid. Place over a high heat and bring to the boil. Reduce the heat slightly and allow to simmer until the potatoes are easily pierced with a sharp knife.

Remove from the heat and allow to cool slightly – it's best to serve the salad warm but not piping hot.

In the meantime, make up the dressing for the potatoes. Pour the tahini, lemon juice, olive oil, water and turmeric into a large bowl and whisk until smooth. If the dressing looks like the oil is splitting out, just add a tablespoon of water at a time until the dressing is thick and glossy. Season with a generous pinch of salt and pepper.

Toss the warm potatoes in the dressing, add the mint leaves and spring onions and mix until thoroughly combined. Tip into a serving bowl and sprinkle the sumac evenly over the top.

SERVES 4–6 AS A SIDE DISH

◇◇◇◇◇◇

# ROAST AUBERGINE
## WITH TOFU AND TURMERIC DENGAKO

This is vegan heaven. Combining the tofu and coconut milk creates a creamy dressing while the miso turmeric dengako glaze gives an umami flavour to the aubergine. It's a salad to impress friends with.

---

2–3 aubergines (depending on size), sliced into 2.5cm rounds
olive oil, for dressing
1 tablespoon white miso
2 tablespoons cooking sake
1 teaspoon ground turmeric
1 tablespoon golden caster sugar
100g kale, tough stems removed and leaves roughly chopped
1 tablespoon soy sauce
1 teaspoon soft light brown sugar
200g firm tofu
50ml coconut milk
sea salt and ground black pepper

**To garnish**
purple basil (optional)
2 tablespoons mixed chopped nuts
pea shoots

Preheat the oven to 230°C (450°F), Gas Mark 8.

Put the aubergine rounds in a large bowl and toss with plenty of olive oil and some sea salt. Arrange the rounds on a large roasting tray.

Whisk the miso, sake, turmeric and sugar together to make a loose paste. Brush over the aubergine slices and roast in the oven for about 20 minutes until soft and deep golden in colour, turning and brushing again with the paste halfway through. Remove from the oven and allow to cool a little.

Meanwhile, toss the kale with a little soy sauce and brown sugar and spread out on a baking tray. As soon as you have removed the aubergine, put the kale in the oven and switch it off to allow the kale to crisp in the residual heat while you arrange the salad.

Blitz the tofu with the coconut milk, either in a food processor or with a hand-held blender, for just a few seconds to create a creamy, crumbly texture.

Arrange the aubergine rounds on a salad platter and scatter over the tofu and then the crispy kale. Finish with some purple basil, if using, chopped nuts, a few pea shoots and a grinding of black pepper.

**SERVES 2**

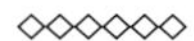

# SWEET POTATO BULGUR

Grain salads are a great choice for a lunchbox or sharing salad platter as the grain makes it feel more filling. You can mix and match your grains and roasted vegetables, for example carrots with freekeh or butternut squash wedges with cracked wheat.

---

- 1 large sweet potato, roughly chopped
- 1½ teaspoons ground turmeric
- 1 teaspoon cumin seeds
- 2–3 tablespoons olive oil
- 100g bulgur wheat
- 1 teaspoon bouillon powder
- 100g baby spinach (shredded) or baby kale
- 2 tablespoons extra virgin olive oil
- zest and juice of ½ lime
- 50ml baked kefir or natural yogurt
- sea salt
- fresh coriander leaves, to serve

Preheat the oven to 220°C (425°F), Gas Mark 7.

Put the potatoes in a large bowl with 1 teaspoon of the ground turmeric, the cumin seeds, olive oil and a good pinch of salt and mix together. Transfer to a roasting tin and roast for about 20 minutes until the sweet potatoes are soft and a little crispy at the edges. Turn halfway through cooking.

Place the bulgur wheat in a saucepan, cover with 1 litre of water and add the bouillon and remaining ground turmeric. Bring to the boil, then reduce the heat and simmer for 10–12 minutes until cooked. Drain.

Toss the bulgur and roast sweet potato together with the spinach or kale and some extra virgin olive oil in a large bowl. Transfer to a salad platter.

Mix the lime zest and juice into the kefir or yogurt and drizzle over the salad, then scatter over the picked coriander leaves. Serve warm or alternatively, leave to cool and then chill in the refrigerator until needed.

**SERVES 6**

# FIVE VEG TAGINE

This recipe does have quite a long list of ingredients, but the process is fairly simple and results in a great depth of flavour. Many of the spices are things that you can keep in your storecupboard, but feel free to mix and match along with the vegetables. This recipe works really well in big batches that you can keep in the refrigerator and then simply heat up later in the week.

---

½ tablespoon ground turmeric
½ tablespoon ground ginger
½ tablespoon dried chilli flakes
½ tablespoon ground cumin
½ tablespoon ground coriander
seeds of 4 cardamom pods
1 garlic clove, crushed
juice of 1 lemon
100ml olive oil
2 carrots, cut into wedges
½ butternut squash, peeled and cut into bite-sized pieces
2 small turnips, cut into wedges
½ celeriac, peeled and cut into bite-sized pieces
1 aubergine, cut into 2cm dice
400g can chickpeas, rinsed and drained
500ml vegetable stock
1 tablespoon tomato purée
sea salt and ground black pepper
couscous and natural yogurt, to serve

Preheat the oven to 200°C (400°F), Gas Mark 6.

Mix together all the spices, garlic, lemon juice and olive oil in a bowl and season with salt and pepper. Add all the vegetables and mix thoroughly.

Place a large flameproof casserole over a medium heat and add the vegetables so that they temper for a few minutes. Now add the chickpeas, vegetable stock and tomato purée. Give everything a stir, cover and put in the oven for 30–40 minutes until the vegetables are cooked and the flavours have all infused.

Prepare your couscous and spoon into bowls. Ladle the tagine over the couscous and serve with a spoonful of natural yogurt on top.

SERVES 2 (OR 4 AS A SIDE)

◇◇◇◇◇◇

# YELLOW RICE
## WITH COCONUT HALLOUMI

This coconut fried halloumi is a winner every time and is a very nice treat with a bowl of hot, steaming yellow rice.

---

zest of 1 lemon
1 teaspoon ground turmeric
1 teaspoon ground ginger
2 teaspoons yellow mustard seeds
150g basmati rice, rinsed
300ml hot vegetable stock
8 kaffir lime leaves
100g halloumi cheese, cubed
flour, for dusting
1 egg, beaten
50g coconut flakes
vegetable oil, for frying
apple blossom flowers, to garnish
(or use mint sprigs)

Dry-fry the lemon zest, turmeric, ginger and yellow mustard seeds in a saucepan until the seeds begin to pop. Add the rice, stock and kaffir lime leaves and bring to the boil, then reduce the heat and simmer for 10 minutes, or until the rice is fluffy and cooked and all the liquid has been absorbed.

For the halloumi, dip the cubes first into some flour, then the beaten egg, then the coconut flakes, pressing to coat on all sides.

Heat the vegetable oil for shallow-frying in a wok and fry the coconut halloumi cubes until golden brown on all sides. Carefully remove with a slotted spoon and place on kitchen paper to drain away the excess oil.

Fluff up the rice with a fork and top with the fried halloumi. Garnish with apple blossom, if using, and serve immediately.

SERVES 4–6 AS A SIDE DISH

◇◇◇◇◇◇

# ROAST CAULIFLOWER SALAD
## WITH GINGER, TURMERIC AND LIME DRESSING

Roasting cauliflower whole is now a popular technique: it's a simple way to cook this versatile vegetable and gives it a lovely sweetness. The turmeric is in the dressing, which you toss the cauliflower in before serving with quinoa and spring onion and fresh coriander to finish.

---

1 medium cauliflower
4 tablespoons olive oil
1 teaspoon yellow mustard seeds
1 teaspoon fennel seeds
1 teaspoon ground coriander
1 teaspoon ground cumin
1 teaspoon ground turmeric
juice of 1 lime
5cm piece of fresh root ginger, peeled and grated
100g mixed quinoa
3 spring onions, thinly sliced on the diagonal
sea salt flakes

**To garnish**
handful of coriander leaves
handful of Thai basil leaves (optional)
Spiced and Roasted Seeds (*see* page 30; optional)

Preheat the oven to 220°C (425°F), Gas Mark 7.

To roast the cauliflower whole, simply place on a roasting tray, drizzle over half the olive oil and sprinkle with sea salt. Roast for 45–60 minutes, or until the cauliflower is golden in colour and can be easily pierced with a sharp knife. Remove from the oven and allow to cool a little before slicing into thick 'steaks'.

Heat the remaining oil in a saucepan and add the mustard seeds, stirring for about 1 minute over a medium-high heat until the seeds begin to pop. Add the fennel seeds, coriander, cumin and turmeric. Cook, stirring, for another minute or so until fragrant. Remove the pan from heat and mix in the lime juice and ginger. Allow to cool and season with salt.

Mix the cauliflower in the dressing in a large bowl (don't worry if the cauliflower breaks up into florets) and leave to marinate while you cook the quinoa according to the packet instructions. Drain and set aside to cool.

Mix the quinoa into the cauliflower and dressing and arrange on a salad platter. Scatter over the sliced spring onion, fresh coriander, Thai basil and spiced and roasted seeds, if using, just before serving.

**SERVES 1**

◇◇◇◇◇◇

# BUDDHA BOWL

The idea of the Buddha bowl is to have something plant-based from each of the main food groups – in other words some protein, good carbohydrates, healthy fats and plenty of fresh veg. With this recipe you get all that goodness plus the added benefits of some turmeric thrown in. The trick here is to cook the individual elements of the bowl separately so that you can enjoy all the layers and flavours.

---

100g cooked Yellow Rice (*see page 64*) or cooked basmati rice
unsalted butter or coconut oil, for frying
1 roasted garlic clove (wrap a whole garlic bulb with sea salt in foil and roast in a low oven for 1 hour)
50g mixed oriental mushrooms
1 tablespoon white wine
½ teaspoon harissa
50g baby spinach
50g green beans
1 teaspoon grated fresh turmeric or ground turmeric
25g firm tofu
1 black radish, scrubbed and thinly sliced
½ teaspoon grated fresh root ginger or ground ginger
¼ Chinese cabbage, shredded
sea salt flakes

Cook the rice and keep warm in a low oven – around 150°C (300°F), Gas Mark 2.

Melt about 1 teaspoon butter or coconut oil in a hot frying pan and squeeze the roasted garlic clove into the pan. Stir for a few moments before adding the mushrooms, tossing continuously until golden and cooked. Deglaze with the white wine, transfer to a bowl and keep warm in the oven with the rice.

In the same pan, fry off the harissa and add the baby spinach to wilt, then toss in the harissa. Set aside.

Heat a little coconut oil in a pan and add the green beans, turmeric and tofu, along with a little salt, scrambling the tofu as you cook the beans. Remove from the pan and set aside.

Last for the veg, melt a little more butter or coconut oil with the grated ginger and wilt the Chinese cabbage for a minute or two.

Assemble your bowl with all the elements and serve.

SERVES 4 AS A SIDE DISH

◇◇◇◇◇◇

# BHINDI MASALA CURRY

This is a lightly spiced North Indian dish using the rather unheralded okra, which you do have to be careful not to overcook as they go slimy. They're delicious in this traditional veg curry.

---

2 tablespoons coconut oil
300g okra, each sliced at an angle into 3–4 pieces
1 large onion, finely diced
1 bay leaf
1 teaspoon ground turmeric
½ teaspoon chilli powder
½ teaspoon ground coriander
½ teaspoon ground cumin
200ml water
10g fresh coriander, chopped
sea salt flakes
rice or Indian bread, to serve

**For the tomato paste**
3 ripe tomatoes
1cm piece of fresh root ginger, peeled and roughly chopped
4 garlic cloves
2 green chillies
2 cloves
½ teaspoon ground cinnamon
2 tablespoons natural yogurt

For the tomato paste, put the tomatoes, ginger, garlic and chillies in a food processor and blend together until completely smooth. Crush the cloves with the cinnamon and add to the paste. Stir in the yogurt and leave to one side.

Melt half the coconut oil in large frying pan over a low heat and fry the okra for 10–15 minutes until almost cooked – still firm but slightly browned all over. Remove from the pan and drain on kitchen paper.

In the same pan, add the remaining coconut oil and fry the onion with the bay leaf until completely soft and slightly caramelized. Add the ground spices and stir quickly so as not to burn them. Stir in the tomato paste and keep cooking over a low heat until the sauce has thickened. Add the water, season with salt and give it a very good stir. Return the okra to the sauce and cook for another 5 minutes. Do not cook for longer otherwise the okra will go extremely slimy.

Add the chopped coriander and serve with rice or a good Indian bread to soak up the sauce.

**SERVES 4**

◇◇◇◇◇◇

# TURMERIC GNOCCHI

Seaweed and turmeric make a surprisingly good combination. You don't need to go to all the trouble of making your own gnocchi to make this recipe but you will notice the difference if you have the time and patience to give it a try.

---

4 large floury potatoes, such as Russet or Desirée
150g plain flour, plus extra for dusting
2 teaspoons sea salt flakes
1 egg, beaten
100g unsalted butter, at room temperature and cut into small cubes
½ teaspoon ground turmeric
1 teaspoon nori or dulse seaweed flakes
1 tablespoon vegetable oil
50g pecorino cheese (or any hard cheese), grated
handful of fresh chives, chopped
2 tablespoons Spiced and Roasted Seeds (*see page 30*) or toasted pumpkin seeds
pea shoots, to garnish
ground black pepper

Preheat the oven to 220°C (425°F), Gas Mark 7.

Bake the potatoes for about 45 minutes, or until easily pierced with a sharp knife. When just cool enough to handle, peel the potatoes and pass through a potato ricer into a bowl. (Alternatively, mash until smooth and then push the mixture through a sieve.) Allow to cool.

Sift the flour into the potatoes and sprinkle over the salt. Create a small well in the middle and add the beaten egg. Stir and mix together before tipping out onto a floured surface. Knead the mixture until it is soft and smooth, then divide in half, then again and once more, so that you have 8 equal pieces. Now roll these into long sausage ropes and cut into pieces about 2cm square.

Bring a saucepan of salted water to the boil and cook the gnocchi in batches – they are ready when they float to the surface, usually after a few minutes. Remove with a slotted spoon and drain on kitchen paper.

When the gnocchi are cooked, melt the butter in a large frying pan and add the turmeric and seaweed flakes. In a separate pan, add the vegetable oil and fry the gnocchi, again in batches, and divide among 4 bowls. Drizzle over the flavoured butter and scatter with grated cheese, chives and toasted seeds. Finish with a few pea shoots and a grinding of black pepper and serve immediately.

# FISH & MEAT DISHES

FEMALE FRIENDLY SOCIETY
DUNTON
BASSETT

SERVES 2

◇◇◇◇◇◇

# TURMERIC PRAWN LINGUINE

This is a wonderful sharing dish. The traditional Mediterranean flavours work really well with the addition of the turmeric and fresh yogurt sauce.

---

- 2 tablespoons olive oil, plus extra for drizzling
- ½ shallot, finely diced
- 1 garlic clove, grated or very finely chopped
- 2.5cm piece of fresh root ginger, peeled and grated
- 1 teaspoon ground turmeric
- 200g raw prawns (ideally shell-on)
- 200g linguine
- 150g natural yogurt
- 50g rocket
- 8 cherry tomatoes, halved
- sea salt and ground black pepper

Fill a large saucepan with water, add a handful of salt and put over a high heat.

While the pasta water is coming to the boil, heat the oil in a frying pan over a low–medium heat. Add the shallot and fry slowly until it becomes transparent. Add the garlic and ginger and continue to fry over a low heat until they are aromatic and soft, about 4–5 minutes. Add the turmeric and cook for another couple of minutes.

Increase the heat and add the prawns, stirring to coat them in the other ingredients, and cook for 4–8 minutes.

By this time, the water should be boiling, so add the linguine and cook according to the packet instructions. Drain the pasta, reserving a cupful of the water, and stir a little oil through it.

Once the prawns feel firm to touch and are pink all over, add the yogurt and a half ladle of reserved pasta water. Cook, stirring, for 3–4 minutes to fully soak up the flavours, adding more water if necessary.

Season to taste and reduce the heat to very low. Add the drained pasta, rocket and tomatoes and stir through until the rocket has wilted. The pasta will soak up the sauce so if it looks a little dry add some more pasta water until you have a sauce that coats every strand. Serve immediately.

**SERVES 2**

◇◇◇◇◇◇

# MISO TURMERIC GLAZED SALMON WITH WILTED GREENS

The glaze for the salmon lifts this simple and healthy weeknight dinner to create something special. Salmon is full of healthy Omega oils, which have a very important role in maintaining cells.

---

- 2 tablespoons mirin
- 1 teaspoon coconut sugar (or use brown sugar)
- 1 garlic clove, roasted (*see* page 68)
- 1 teaspoon brown miso paste
- 1 teaspoon Turmeric Honey (*see* page 15, or use clear honey)
- 1 tablespoon light sesame oil
- 2 x 150g skin-on salmon fillets
- 1 tablespoon unsalted butter
- ½ teaspoon ground turmeric
- ⅛ teaspoon ground black pepper
- 1 bok choy, leaves separated
- 100g mangetout
- 100g cavolo nero, stalks removed and leaves chopped
- few slices of sushi ginger
- 2 tablespoons soy sauce

To make the glaze, whisk together the mirin, sugar, garlic, miso paste and honey.

Preheat the grill to high. Place a nonstick frying pan (with a heatproof handle) over a medium–high heat, add the sesame oil and fry the salmon skin side down until the skin is golden and crisp. Turn over, brush with the miso turmeric glaze and place the pan under the grill for a few minutes.

Heat another large frying pan or wok over a high heat and add the butter, turmeric and black pepper. Add the bok choy, mangetout and cavolo nero. Toss for about 30 seconds, then add the sushi ginger and soy sauce.

When the greens are wilted, divide between 2 plates and top with the glazed salmon.

**SERVES 2**

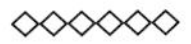

# KERALAN FISH CURRY

With the combination of spices, this is a gentle but warming curry from the Ayurvedic tradition, balanced by the coconut milk and lemon. It's a lovely fresh dish and you can use any firm, white-fleshed fish that is in season.

---

1 tablespoon groundnut oil
2.5cm piece of cinnamon stick
3 cloves
⅓ teaspoon mustard seeds
⅓ teaspoon fennel seeds
5 black peppercorns
½ onion, thinly sliced
7 dried curry leaves
150g basmati rice
1½ teaspoons garlic paste
1½ teaspoons ginger paste
¼ teaspoon ground turmeric
pinch of sea salt
100ml water
100ml coconut milk
squeeze of lemon juice
250g firm monkfish (or cod), cut into large cubes
1 teaspoon unsalted butter or coconut oil
80g monk's beard or samphire (or use baby spinach)

Heat the oil in a large nonstick saucepan, add the whole spices and cook over a medium heat until the mustard seeds start popping. Add the onion and curry leaves and cook for a few minutes until soft and translucent.

Meanwhile, cook the rice according to the packet instructions.

Add the garlic and ginger pastes to the spices and stir for a minute. Add the turmeric, salt and water. Bring to the boil, then reduce the heat and simmer for about 7 minutes until nicely reduced. Add the coconut milk, bring back to the boil and cook for a couple of minutes.

Squeeze in the lemon juice and add the fish in one layer, just covering with the sauce. Simmer gently until the fish is cooked through, about 8 minutes (depending on the thickness of the fish). Taste for seasoning.

Heat the butter or coconut oil in a pan and sauté the monks beard or samphire for a minute or two.

Serve the curry on the rice with greens scattered over.

SERVES 2

◇◇◇◇◇◇

# TURMERIC AND TAMARIND COD

This recipe marries the turmeric with the cod and the honey in the salad dressing. The salad is raw, giving freshness and crunch to complement the gently cooked fish.

---

1 tablespoon tamarind paste
½ teaspoon grated fresh turmeric or ground turmeric
1 tablespoon hot water
2 x 200g skin-on cod fillet pieces (ask the fishmonger to remove any bones)
½ onion, grated
good splash of rose or jasmine tea
lime wedges, to serve

**For the salad**
½ white cabbage, finely chopped or grated
½ small cucumber (ideally Lebanese), sliced
½ red onion, thinly sliced
handful of any soft fresh herbs, such as basil, mint, dill
1 teaspoon black onion seeds
2 teaspoons manuka honey (or use raw honey)
3 tablespoons natural yogurt
sea salt and ground black pepper

Mix the tamarind paste, turmeric and hot water together in a large bowl until combined and allow to cool. Toss the fish in the marinade, then add the grated onion and chill in the refrigerator for 20 minutes.

Mix together all of the salad ingredients in a bowl until well combined. Season with salt and pepper and leave to one side.

Get a nonstick pan really hot and then place the cod skin side down in the pan. Cook for 3 minutes, then turn the fish over and add a splash of tea. After the initial whoosh sound of the tea hitting the pan, reduce the heat, cover the pan and steam for about 5 minutes.

Pile the salad onto plates and serve the fish on top with lime wedges for squeezing.

SERVES 4

◇◇◇◇◇◇

# MUSSELS
## WITH TURMERIC AND LEMON GRASS

Mussels are wonderful for sharing and so simple to cook. They can take on lots of strong flavours, in this case the combination of turmeric, chilli and lemon grass works beautifully.

---

- 2 tablespoons coconut oil
- 4 garlic cloves, sliced
- 2 red chillies, deseeded and thinly sliced
- 1 lemon grass stalk, crushed along the stem and halved
- ½ teaspoon ground turmeric
- 1kg fresh mussels, cleaned and de-bearded
- 400g cherry tomatoes, halved
- 1 bunch of fresh Thai basil (or use red basil or regular basil)
- sea salt and ground black pepper

Heat the coconut oil in a large, wide saucepan with a lid over a low–medium heat and add the garlic, chillies and lemon grass. Fry for a few minutes until they are aromatic and the garlic begins to brown slightly. Add the turmeric and cook for another 30 seconds.

Increase the heat to high and add the mussels and tomatoes. Season with salt and pepper, stir all together and cover the pan. Shake every now and again so the mussels are nudged open – this should take around 4–5 minutes.

Give the last few mussels a chance to open if they haven't already but if any remain firmly shut, make sure you discard them before serving. When they're all opened you should have a lovely broth at the bottom made from the mussel and tomato juices.

Serve in a large sharing platter with plenty of Thai basil scattered over.

SERVES 4

◇◇◇◇◇◇

# BEEF STEW

Adding turmeric to stews is a simple way to add a little more of this healthy spice into your cooking. With the ginger, it adds a touch of warmth to this hearty beef stew. Feel free to use any seasonal root veg and tubers you have to hand (parsnips, squash, swede, celeriac).

---

olive oil, for frying
2 onions, sliced
400g stewing steak, cut into chunks and seasoned with salt and pepper
1 teaspoon ground turmeric
1 teaspoon ground ginger
6 shallots, halved
12 baby carrots
8 baby turnips
1 litre vegetable stock (or enough to cover the meat)
Parmesan cheese rind (if to hand)
hunks of sourdough bread, to serve

Preheat the oven to 150°C (300°F), Gas Mark 2.

Heat a little olive oil in a large flameproof casserole and add the onions. Gently fry over a low–medium heat until softened. Remove from the casserole, add a little more oil and start browning the steak in batches.

Return the meat and the onions to the casserole, add the turmeric and ginger, then cook slowly for 10 minutes.

Add the shallots, carrots, turnips, vegetable stock and Parmesan rind, if using. Cover and place in the oven for 3 hours. Check on it occasionally to make sure there is enough liquid to cover the meat and vegetables. If at any time it looks dryish, top it up with stock or a little water.

Serve with hunks of crusty sourdough bread to mop up the flavoursome juices.

SERVES 4

# MASSAMAN BEEF LARB

Larb is a South-East Asian dish that is particularly popular in Laos and is made with mince and served in lettuce leaves. In this recipe it is deconstructed and paired with the fragrant massaman Thai curry paste. You can buy massaman paste in the supermarket but, for a really fresh taste, why not make your own? You can also use any type of mince you like as an alternative to beef – pork, chicken or duck would all work well.

---

400g minced beef, seasoned with salt and pepper
1 tablespoon massaman paste (*see* below)
1 tablespoon groundnut oil
2 shallots, chopped
100ml hot vegetable stock
200g couscous
1 tablespoon extra virgin olive oil

**For the massaman paste (makes 1 small jar)**
8 garlic cloves
2 lemon grass stalks, outer layers removed and thinly sliced
1 shallot, sliced
2.5cm piece of fresh root ginger, peeled and sliced
1 tablespoon sesame oil
seeds of 4 cardamom pods
1 tablespoon coriander seeds
1 teaspoon cumin seeds

First make the paste. Preheat the oven to 180°C (350°F), Gas Mark 4 and toss the garlic, lemon grass, shallot and ginger with the sesame oil. Spread out over a baking tray and roast for 8 minutes, tossing halfway. Allow to cool.

Meanwhile, combine the cardamom, coriander and cumin seeds in a small nonstick pan and toast over a medium heat until fragrant, about 2 minutes. Allow the spices to cool before crushing them in a spice mill or with a pestle and mortar.

Tip the roasted garlic, lemon grass, shallot and ginger into a food processor and add the ground spices and all the remaining paste ingredients. Blitz to a paste, adding a little olive oil if the mixture is too dry. The paste can be made in advance and kept in the refrigerator for up to a month.

Tip the minced beef into a large bowl, add the tablespoon of massaman paste and mix together. Leave to marinate for 30 minutes, if you have time.

1 teaspoon ground turmeric
½ teaspoon ground cinnamon
¼ teaspoon ground cloves
½ teaspoon sea salt flakes
small bunch of fresh coriander stems
1 teaspoon chilli paste (or to taste)

**To serve**
mixed salad leaves
fresh picked thyme
Turmeric-infused Oil (*see* page 37)

Heat the oil in a large frying pan and sauté the shallots over a medium heat until soft, about 5 minutes. Remove and set aside while you brown the mince in the same pan. Once the mince is browned, return the onions to the pan along with the hot vegetable stock and simmer for 15–20 minutes.

Put the couscous in a large bowl and add enough just-boiled water to just cover. Drizzle in a little extra virgin olive oil and cover with clingfilm or a plate for 5 minutes until the couscous has absorbed the water and can be easily fluffed with a fork.

Serve the couscous and larb with lots of fresh salad leaves and fresh thyme. Drizzle over a little turmeric oil to finish.

**SERVES 4**

◇◇◇◇◇◇

# ROAST CHICKEN
## WITH TANDOORI RUB

The spices in this rub result in a subtle flavour that is not too heavy or overpowering, so this is definitely one to try for Sunday lunch or the next time you want to roast a whole chicken.

---

1 large whole chicken
1 lemon
400g purple sprouting broccoli
olive oil, for drizzling
½ teaspoon dried chilli flakes
100g baby kale or baby leaf salad
sea salt flakes

**For the brine (optional)**
4.5 litres cold water
85g fine salt
200g soft light brown sugar

**For the tandoori paste**
2 tablespoons coconut oil
½ teaspoon ground ginger
1 teaspoon ground cumin
1 teaspoon garam masala
½ teaspoon chilli powder
½ teaspoon ground coriander
1 teaspoon ground turmeric
½ teaspoon ground black pepper
3 garlic cloves, crushed

Whisk all the brine ingredients together until dissolved. Put the chicken into a stockpot or container big enough to hold the chicken comfortably. Pour over enough of the brine to cover it entirely. Leave for at least 3 hours but ideally overnight. Remove the chicken from the brine, rinse and pat dry with kitchen paper. (You can skip the brining step if you are cooking on the day.)

Preheat the oven to 200°C (400°F), Gas Mark 6.

Pound or blend all the paste ingredients together so you have a thick-ish rub.

Slice the lemon into four and rub the chicken all over, inside and out. Rub the paste all over the chicken, making sure you don't neglect the legs, thighs and wings.

Put the lemon quarters into the cavity, place the chicken in a roasting tray and cover with foil. Roast in the oven for 2 hours, then remove the foil, increase the heat to 240°C (475°F), Gas Mark 9 and cook for another 20 minutes, or until well browned. Remove from the oven and allow to rest.

Steam the broccoli until cooked but still with some bite. Toss with a little olive oil, the chilli flakes and some sea salt. Serve the chicken with the broccoli and kale salad.

**SERVES 2**

◇◇◇◇◇◇

# LAMB CUTLETS
## IN TURMERIC COCONUT MARINADE

The turmeric coconut marinade used in this recipe infuses the meat with delicious flavours that perfectly complement the richness of the lamb. This is a stunning dish for cooking on the barbecue at the height of summer and is great served with a crisp, fresh, mixed leaf salad scattered with spiced and roasted seeds (*see* page 30). You could even drizzle your salad with a dressing based on the turmeric-infused oil on page 37.

---

4 lamb cutlets (about 100g each)
mixed leaf salad, to serve
Spiced and Roasted Seeds (*see* page 30), to serve

**For the marinade**
70g creamed coconut
juice of ½ lemon
2 tablespoons vegetable oil
4 tablespoons water
20g fresh coriander, roughly chopped
½ shallot, quartered
2 garlic cloves
½ teaspoon ground cumin
½ teaspoon ground coriander
1½ teaspoons ground turmeric

Melt the creamed coconut in a saucepan over a low heat until it has become a liquid again. Add to a bowl with the remaining marinade ingredients and whisk them all together until you have a thick, rich, glossy marinade. If the oils are splitting, adding a little water or lemon juice will bring it back together again. You should end up with a beautiful yellow paste flecked with coriander.

Coat the lamb cutlets in the marinade and then transfer the cutlets and all the marinade to a non-metallic container or resealable plastic food bag and place in the refrigerator overnight to absorb the flavours. Technically the longer the better, so you can leave them for up to 3 days in the refrigerator if you're planning ahead.

When you are ready to cook, make sure you take the cutlets out of the refrigerator well before you start cooking as you want them to come to room temperature so the marinade melts again.

For the best results, a barbecue will cook the perfect lamb cutlets but otherwise a griddle pan is perfect.

Heat the pan to smoking point and then reduce the heat to medium. After a couple of minutes, add the lamb cutlets. Do not touch them so they get lovely char marks – if you move them too much they will never brown in a nice uniform way. Once they have char marks on the one side, flip them over and do the same again, increasing the heat if the pan has cooled slightly.

They are ready when both sides have nice char marks and the meat next to the bone is springy and slightly firm. Remove from the heat, cover with foil and leave to rest for at least 5 minutes.

Serve the lamb simply with a mixed leaf salad and some spiced and roasted seeds.

# SWEETS

MAKES 1 LITRE

◇◇◇◇◇◇

# TURMERIC MAPLE ICE CREAM

This is a cheat's recipe as you don't need an ice cream machine to make it. If you do have a machine, then you can use your favourite base recipe and add the maple syrup and turmeric to flavour your ice cream. It's surprising but the turmeric really works with the cream.

---

30g maple syrup
1 teaspoon ground turmeric
600ml double cream
397g can condensed milk
4 caramelized biscuits (such as Lotus Biscoff), crushed into fine crumbs

Gently heat the maple syrup and turmeric together in a small saucepan for a few minutes, just to infuse the flavours. Put to one side to cool.

Put the cream and condensed milk into a large bowl and, using a hand-held electric whisk, beat for 5 minutes or so until the mixture forms soft peaks.

Whisk the turmeric-infused maple syrup into the cream and condensed milk mixture, then spoon into a rigid freezerproof container.

Freeze overnight until firm. Transfer to the refrigerator for 15–20 minutes before scooping. Serve with the biscuit crumbs scattered over.

MAKES 1 BIG BOWL

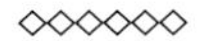

# POPCORN

This is such a simple but popular snack – if you prefer savoury to sweet, then just replace the maple syrup with ½ teaspoon ground cumin.

---

2 tablespoons coconut oil
200g popcorn kernels
½ teaspoon ground turmeric
¼ teaspoon dried chilli flakes
1 teaspoon sea salt flakes (or to taste)
2 tablespoons maple syrup

Place a large, deep, lidded saucepan over a high heat. When the pan is hot, add the coconut oil and after about 30 seconds add the popcorn kernels.

Cover the pan and shake so that the kernels are all getting the heat as they pop. It's a bit tricky to know when all the kernels have popped if you don't have a glass lid, but when the popping noise stops, have a look.

Tip into a bowl and sprinkle over the turmeric, dried chilli flakes and sea salt. Drizzle over the maple syrup and shake until the seasoning is evenly distributed. Serve immediately.

MAKES 8 MUFFINS

◇◇◇◇◇◇

# TURMERIC CHAI MUFFINS

These muffins aren't super sweet and have a lovely soft texture, making them perfect for a weekend treat.

---

50g unsalted butter, softened
120g golden caster sugar
1 egg
½ teaspoon vanilla extract
175g plain flour
½ teaspoon salt
¾ teaspoon baking powder
¼ teaspoon bicarbonate of soda
1 teaspoon ground cinnamon
½ teaspoon ground turmeric
½ teaspoon ground ginger
½ teaspoon ground cardamom
¼ teaspoon ground black pepper
100ml milk (or nut milk of choice)

**For the glaze**
25g butter, melted
60g icing sugar, sifted
2 teaspoons milk (or nut milk of choice)
¼ teaspoon ground cinnamon
pinch of ground ginger
pinch of ground turmeric
pinch of ground cardamom
¼ teaspoon vanilla extract

Preheat the oven to 180°C (350°F), Gas Mark 4 and line a muffin tray with 8 paper cases.

Cream the butter and sugar in a large bowl with a wooden spoon until pale and fluffy. Gradually add the egg and vanilla extract and mix until fully incorporated.

In a separate bowl, mix all the dry ingredients together including the spices. Add half the dry ingredients to the egg and sugar mixture and mix until fully combined. Add half the milk and mix in before adding and mixing the remaining dry ingredients. Finally incorporate the rest of the milk until you have a smooth mixture.

Spoon this mixture into each muffin case almost to the top. Bake for around 20–25 minutes, or until the tops of the muffins are well risen and spring back when touched (or check with a skewer). Transfer to a wire rack to cool.

Meanwhile, combine all the glaze ingredients until smooth. Once the muffins have cooled slightly, after 5–10 minutes, dip their tops into the glaze and wait until it hardens. They can then be double-dipped if desired for extra flavour. Alternatively, you can drizzle the glaze over the tops of the muffins with a spoon.

SERVES 10–12

◇◇◇◇◇◇

# MANGO AND TURMERIC NO-BAKE CHEESECAKE

This delicious tropical cheesecake looks amazing, with its cheery mango purée topping, and is really easy to make, requiring no baking whatsoever. A slice of this makes the perfect dessert after a curry as the cream cheese has a cooling effect on the palate. The health-conscious among you may wish to use reduced-fat cream cheese instead of full-fat. Either way, this cake is a real showstopper.

---

**For the base**
250g gingersnap biscuits
¼ teaspoon ground black pepper
100g salted butter, melted

**For the filling**
1 large mango
2½ teaspoons ground turmeric
400g full-fat cream cheese (or use reduced-fat)
100g caster sugar
250ml double cream
4 tablespoons water
1 tablespoon powdered gelatine

Base-line a 20cm round springform cake tin with baking paper.

Make the base by blitzing the gingersnap biscuits and black pepper in a food processor until a fine crumb is reached. Add the melted butter and stir until it is all incorporated. Press this mixture firmly into the bottom of the cake tin with the back of a spoon and chill in the refrigerator for at least 30 minutes.

Make a mango purée by peeling the mango and blitzing all of its flesh in a food processor until it is smooth and free of chunks. Add ½ teaspoon of the ground turmeric to the purée and mix well.

In a bowl, beat the cream cheese, sugar and remaining turmeric by hand with a spatula or wooden spoon until the sugar has dissolved. In a separate bowl, whisk the cream until soft peaks form. Put to one side.

Bloom the gelatine by putting 4 tablespoons of cold water into a small pan (this can also be done in a

microwave in a plastic bowl). Slowly sprinkle the gelatine onto the surface of the water and wait 5 minutes until it has absorbed the water and formed a slushy paste. Warm this paste over a very low heat, just to melt the gelatine, stirring with a fork continuously until the gelatine granules have fully dissolved. Once the granules have dissolved, take the liquid off the heat and whisk into the mango purée.

Whisk two-thirds of the mango purée into the cream cheese mixture, then carefully fold in the whipped cream until fully incorporated. Pour this mixture onto the chilled biscuit base and smooth down the top with a palette knife. Return to the refrigerator to chill for 1–2 hours.

Once the cheesecake has almost set, finish it by pouring the remaining mango purée over the top and smoothing it down with a palette knife. Chill the cake for 2 hours, or until fully set before cutting and serving.

**SERVES 2**

◇◇◇◇◇◇

# TURMERIC-GLAZED BANANA
## WITH ICE CREAM

This is the simplest of desserts – the turmeric complements the sweetness of the banana and maple to give just the right balance.

---

- 2 tablespoons unsalted butter
- 1 teaspoon grated fresh turmeric
- 1 large or 2 small bananas, peeled and sliced in half lengthways
- 2 tablespoons maple syrup
- 2 scoops of vanilla ice cream or coconut yogurt

Place a large frying pan over a medium heat and add the butter. When bubbling hot, add the turmeric followed by the bananas, cut sides down. Allow to colour in the butter and turmeric. After a couple of minutes, add the maple syrup to thicken the sauce.

Serve hot with a scoop of vanilla ice cream or coconut yogurt on the side.

SERVES 6

◇◇◇◇◇◇

# COCONUT RICE PUDDING WITH TURMERIC, LEMON GRASS AND GINGER SYRUP

This is a bit of a twist on the traditional rice pudding – the simple addition of coconut, turmeric, lemon grass and ginger make it spiced and sweet at the same time.

---

2 x 400ml cans coconut milk
200ml water
130g Arborio or basmati rice, washed and drained
110g palm sugar or soft light brown sugar
1 lemon grass stalk, ends trimmed and outer layers removed and discarded

**For the syrup**
375ml water
1 teaspoon ground turmeric
2 lemon grass stalks, prepared as above
2.5cm piece of stem ginger, thickly sliced into 4
pared rind of 1 lime (keep the lime to be used later)
pinch of ground black pepper
80g palm sugar or soft light brown sugar

**To garnish (optional)**
apple blossom flowers
few sprigs of lemon verbena

Start by making the syrup. Put the water, turmeric, lemon grass, ginger, lime rind and pepper in a small saucepan and bring to the boil. Reduce to a simmer and let the syrup bubble away for 5–10 minutes, or until reduced by half.

Once reduced, strain the syrup into a bowl, discarding the contents of the sieve. Return the syrup to the pan, add the sugar and bring this to the boil. Reduce this for about 5 minutes until a syrupy consistency is achieved. Cool the syrup and then add 1–2 teaspoons of lime juice to taste. Set the syrup aside.

Put the coconut milk and water in a medium pan and bring to the boil, then add the rice, sugar and lemon grass, stirring well. As soon as the liquid returns to the boil, reduce the heat to medium and cook the rice slowly for about 20 minutes, stirring occasionally so as not to scald the bottom of the pan. Once the rice is cooked but still 'al dente', take the pan off the heat and remove and discard the lemon grass stalk.

Serve the rice pudding warm or cold, topped with a spoonful of the spiced syrup and garnished with apple blossom flowers and lemon verbena sprigs, if liked.

# DRINKS

MAKES 750ML

◇◇◇◇◇◇

# APPLE TURMERIC TONIC

There is something incredibly refreshing about adding the slightly bitter turmeric and sharp lemon juice to sweet apple juice. For an extra shot of goodness, add a few drops of holy basil tincture, an adaptogen that helps your body to cope better with stress.

---

- 750ml pressed apple juice
- 3 teaspoons grated fresh turmeric
- 3 teaspoons grated fresh root ginger
- juice of 2 lemons

Put all the ingredients into a large jug or bowl and allow the flavours to infuse for a few hours, or overnight if possible.

Strain into a large glass bottle and chill in the refrigerator, where it will keep for up to 3 days.

Give the bottle a good shake before serving.

MAKES 500ML

◇◇◇◇◇◇

# CARROT AND ORANGE TONIC

Another refreshing chilled tonic that instantly makes you feel good in the morning.

---

- 300ml fresh squeezed orange juice
- 175ml fresh squeezed carrot juice
- juice of 2 lemons
- 2 teaspoons grated fresh turmeric or ground turmeric
- 2 teaspoons grated fresh root ginger

Put all the ingredients into a large jug or bowl and allow to infuse for a few hours or overnight.

Strain into a large glass bottle and chill in the refrigerator, where it will keep for up to 3 days.

SERVES 1

◇◇◇◇◇◇

# HOT TONIC

For a warming, health-boosting drink, add a little turmeric, some fresh root ginger, lemon slices and raw honey to hot water. Fresh turmeric root is ideal for this infusion, but you can also use ground turmeric if you're having difficulty sourcing the fresh stuff.

---

- 3 thin slices of fresh turmeric or ½ teaspoon ground turmeric
- 3 slices of fresh root ginger
- 2 slices of lemon
- 1 teaspoon raw honey

If using fresh turmeric, simply put all the ingredients in a mug and pour over boiling water. Stir to dissolve the honey and allow the flavours to infuse for 5 minutes before drinking.

If using ground turmeric, add the turmeric and ginger to a small pan of water, bring to the boil and simmer for a few minutes. You might want to add a pinch of black pepper or cayenne pepper. Take off the heat and pour into a mug, adding the lemon and honey. Stir and enjoy.

**MAKES 500ML**

# TURMERIC TODDY

Thyme is good for relieving a sore throat and combines well with the ginger, turmeric, honey and lime in this hot tonic to boost your immune system – delicious any time but especially if you feel the onset of a cold. If you're feeling brave, add a couple of crushed garlic cloves at the same time as the honey.

---

- 10g fresh thyme sprigs
- 1cm piece of fresh root ginger, peeled and grated
- 1 teaspoon grated fresh turmeric or ground turmeric
- ¼ teaspoon black peppercorns
- 500ml water
- 2 tablespoons raw honey
- juice of 1 lime

Use a rolling pin to lightly bash the thyme, which will help to release the oil.

Add the thyme, ginger, turmeric, peppercorns and measured water to a saucepan and bring to just below the boil. Reduce the heat to low and simmer for 10 minutes.

Remove from the heat and add the honey and lime juice, stirring until the honey is dissolved. Strain and serve.

MAKES 1 LARGE POT

# TURMERIC TEA

This is a wonderfully refreshing tea, perfect to start the day with or as a pick-me-up in the afternoon. The addition of cinnamon makes it lovely and warming, although you could replace with a teaspoon of green tea leaves as an alternative. For even more of a chai taste, replace the lemon grass with a few cloves and bashed cardamom pods.

---

1 litre water
½ cinnamon stick
1 lemon grass stalk, bashed
few slices of fresh root ginger
few slices of fresh turmeric or
1 heaped teaspoon ground turmeric
¼ teaspoon black peppercorns

Bring the measured water to the boil in a large saucepan.

Slowly add the herbs and spices and simmer gently for 10 minutes.

Strain into a teapot and serve.

**SERVES 1**

◇◇◇◇◇◇

# GOLDEN MYLK

This is a traditional drink enjoyed in Indonesia. You can try it with or without the cinnamon, depending on your taste. Equally, you might prefer it without any maple syrup or honey.

---

300ml almond or coconut milk
½ teaspoon ground turmeric
½ teaspoon ground cinnamon
pinch of ground black pepper
1 teaspoon coconut oil
1 teaspoon maple syrup (or honey)

Put the almond or coconut milk into a pan and heat gently over a low heat.

Meanwhile, put the remaining ingredients in a small bowl, add a little boiled water and stir to make a paste. Whisk this into the warming milk and then continue to heat gently for 5 minutes. It's then ready to serve.

SERVES 1

◇◇◇◇◇◇

# TURMERIC CHAMPAGNE

This is a twist on a classic cocktail, the turmeric giving it a lovely golden hue. There is no shaking involved here – just build the cocktail in the glass.

---

1 sugar cube
1 teaspoon turmeric juice (extracted from fresh turmeric root)
2 dashes of angostura bitters
1 tablespoon brandy
squeeze of lemon juice
Champagne, to top up
physalis or strip of lemon rind, to garnish

Put the sugar cube in the bottom of a Champagne flute and add the remaining ingredients one at a time.

Garnish the glass with a physalis (or a strip of lemon rind) and enjoy.

SERVES 1

◇◇◇◇◇◇

# TURMERIC WITH PASSION FRUIT

This refreshing cocktail is perfect enjoyed al fresco on a sultry summer's evening.

---

50ml gin
25ml passion fruit and mango purée
20ml sugar syrup
1 tablespoon turmeric juice (see above)
squeeze of lemon juice
passion fruit and lime wedge, to garnish

Put the gin, passion fruit and mango purée, sugar syrup, turmeric juice and lemon juice in a cocktail shaker and shake for about 20 seconds.

Strain into a glass full of ice, garnish with passion fruit and a lime wedge and enjoy.

# BEAUTY

MAKES 1 SMALL POT

◇◇◇◇◇◇

# TURMERIC AND MILK FACE MASK

Due to its antibacterial, anti-inflammatory and antioxidant properties, turmeric isn't just good for cooking with; it can be used as a beauty ingredient, too. The antiseptic and antibacterial properties are particularly beneficial for acne or blemish-prone skin, while the anti-inflammatory nature of turmeric makes it helpful for rosacea. It is important to use organic non-dyed turmeric for these recipes.

---

- 4 tablespoons rice flour
- 2 teaspoons organic ground turmeric
- 6 tablespoons milk or yogurt

Mix all the ingredients together in a small bowl until well combined.

To use, cleanse your face and, while still a little damp, apply the mask to your face, avoiding the eye area. Relax and allow to dry for about 5 minutes and then rinse off thoroughly with lukewarm water.

MAKES 1 SMALL POT

◇◇◇◇◇◇

# TURMERIC AND COCONUT OIL FACE MASK

Coconut oil, like turmeric, is known for its beauty properties, so here is a mask combining both of these natural anti-agers.

---

½ tablespoon organic ground turmeric
1 tablespoon raw honey
3 tablespoons extra virgin coconut oil, melted

Mix all the ingredients together to make a paste. Apply to your (cleansed) face, avoiding the eye area and leave for 10 minutes. Rinse off with lukewarm water and a clean facecloth.

MAKES 1 SMALL POT

◇◇◇◇◇◇

# BODY SCRUB

This scrub is excellent for removing dead skin cells and gently exfoliating the skin, leaving it feeling a little more radiant and youthful.

---

½ tablespoon organic ground turmeric
4 tablespoons brown sugar
melted coconut oil

Mix the turmeric and sugar together and then add enough melted coconut oil, stirring, until you get the consistency of a body scrub.

In the shower, step aside from the water flow to apply the scrub to wet skin. Rub gently all over and then rinse off straightaway in the shower.

# INDEX


**A**

almond milk
- golden mylk 117

angostura bitters
- turmeric Champagne 118

apple
- apple turmeric tonic 111
- bliss balls 28

aubergines
- roast aubergine with tofu and turmeric dengako 61

avocado
- devilled scrambled eggs with avocado on toast 20

**B**

bacon and egg-drop miso 47

bananas
- turmeric banana bread 34
- turmeric-glazed banana with ice cream 104

beans
- kitchari 45

beauty recipes
- body scrub 125
- turmeric and coconut oil face mask 124
- turmeric and milk face mask 123

beef
- beef stew 86
- massaman beef larb 88–9

bhindi masala curry 70

Bircher muesli with turmeric honey 15

bliss balls 28

body scrub 125

bok choy
- miso turmeric glazed salmon with wilted greens 78

brandy
- turmeric Champagne 118

broccoli
- roast chicken with tandoori rub 90

Buddha bowl 68

bulgur
- sweet potato bulgur 62

butter
- corn on the cob with turmeric butter 57

**C**

carrots
- beef stew 86
- carrot and orange tonic 111
- ginger and turmeric carrot soup 42

cashew nuts
- coconut and cashew granola 16

cauliflower
- roast cauliflower salad with ginger, turmeric and lime dressing 67

cavolo nero
- frittata 23
- miso turmeric glazed salmon with wilted greens 78

chai muffins, turmeric 100

Champagne, turmeric 118

cheese
- frittata 23
- turmeric gnocchi 71
- yellow rice with coconut halloumi 64

cheesecake
- mango and turmeric no-bake cheesecake 102–3

chicken
- chicken khai soi 48–9
- coconut chicken soup with turmeric and kale 52
- roast chicken with tandoori rub 90

chickpeas
- five veg tagine 63
- turmeric hummus 33

chillies
- mussels with turmeric and lemon grass 83

cinnamon
- turmeric tea 114

coconut
- coconut and cashew granola 16
- coconut chicken soup with turmeric and kale 52
- lamb cutlets in turmeric coconut marinade 92–3
- squash and coconut dhal 46
- yellow rice with coconut halloumi 64

coconut milk
- coconut rice pudding with turmeric, lemon grass and ginger syrup 105
- golden mylk 117
- roast aubergine with tofu and turmeric dengako 61

cod
- Keralan fish curry 81
- turmeric and tamarind cod 82

corn on the cob with turmeric butter 57

couscous
- massaman beef larb 88–9

cream
- mango and turmeric no-bake cheesecake 102–3
- turmeric maple ice cream 97

cucumber
- turmeric and tamarind cod 82

**D**

devilled scrambled eggs with avocado on toast 20

**E**

eggs
- bacon and egg-drop miso 47

devilled scrambled eggs with avocado on toast 20
frittata 23

F
face masks
turmeric and coconut oil face mask 124
turmeric and milk face mask 123
fish
Keralan fish curry 81
five veg tagine 63
frittata 23

G
gin
turmeric with passion fruit 118
ginger
apple turmeric tonic 111
coconut rice pudding with turmeric, lemon grass and ginger syrup 105
ginger and turmeric carrot soup 42
hot tonic 112
roast cauliflower salad with ginger, turmeric and lime dressing 67
turmeric toddy 113
golden mylk 117

H
honey
Bircher muesli with turmeric honey 15
bliss balls 28
turmeric and tamarind cod 82
turmeric toddy 113
hot tonic 112
hummus, turmeric 33

I
ice cream
turmeric maple ice cream 97
turmeric-glazed banana with ice cream 104

K
kale
coconut chicken soup with turmeric and kale 52
rasam with sashimi and wilting greens 51
roast chicken with tandoori rub 90
Keralan fish curry 81
kitchari 45

L
lamb cutlets in turmeric coconut marinade 92–3
lemon grass
coconut rice pudding with turmeric, lemon grass and ginger syrup 105
mussels with turmeric and lemon grass 83
turmeric tea 114
lemons
apple turmeric tonic 111
carrot and orange tonic 111
hot tonic 112
lime
roast cauliflower salad with ginger, turmeric and lime dressing 67
turmeric toddy 113

M
mackerel
smoked mackerel turmeric congee 24
mangetout
miso turmeric glazed salmon with wilted greens 78
mango
mango and turmeric no-bake cheesecake 102–3
turmeric with passion fruit 118
maple syrup
popcorn 99
turmeric maple ice cream 97
turmeric-glazed banana with ice cream 104
massaman beef larb 88–9
miso
bacon and egg-drop miso 47
miso turmeric glazed salmon with wilted greens 78
monkfish
Keralan fish curry 81
muesli with turmeric honey 15
muffins
turmeric chai muffins 100
mushrooms
Buddha bowl 68
smoked mackerel turmeric congee 24
mussels with turmeric and lemon grass 83
mustard, turmeric 37

N
new potato salad with turmeric tahini dressing 58

O
oats
Bircher muesli with turmeric honey 15
coconut and cashew granola 16
turmeric and black pepper oatcakes 31
oil, turmeric-infused 37
okra
bhindi masala curry 70
onions
beef stew 86
crispy onions 45
oranges
carrot and orange tonic 111

P
passion fruit
turmeric with passion fruit 118
pasta
turmeric prawn linguine 77
peas, split
squash and coconut dhal 46
pepper, black 8
golden mylk 117
turmeric and black pepper oatcakes 31

pickles, turmeric 36
popcorn 99
potatoes
new potato salad with turmeric tahini dressing 58
turmeric gnocchi 71
prawn linguine, turmeric 77

**Q**

quinoa
roast cauliflower salad with ginger, turmeric and lime dressing 67

**R**

rasam with sashimi and wilting greens 51
rice
Buddha bowl 68
coconut rice pudding with turmeric, lemon grass and ginger syrup 105
Keralan fish curry 81
smoked mackerel turmeric congee 24
yellow rice with coconut halloumi 64
roast aubergine with tofu and turmeric dengako 61
roast cauliflower salad with ginger, turmeric and lime dressing 67
roast chicken with tandoori rub 90

**S**

salmon
miso turmeric glazed salmon with wilted greens 78
rasam with sashimi and wilting greens 51
samphire
Keralan fish curry 81
seaweed
kitchari 45
turmeric gnocchi 71
seeds
coconut and cashew granola 16
kitchari 45
spiced and roasted seeds 30
smoked mackerel turmeric congee 24
spiced and roasted seeds 30
spinach
rasam with sashimi and wilting greens 51
squash and coconut dhal 46
sweet potato bulgur 62

**T**

tahini
new potato salad with turmeric tahini dressing 58
tamarind
turmeric and tamarind cod 82
tea
turmeric tea 114
thyme
turmeric toddy 113
tofu
Buddha bowl 68
roast aubergine with tofu and turmeric dengako 61
tomatoes
bhindi masala curry 70
turmeric prawn linguine 77
turmeric 6–7
dosage 8
health benefits 7–8
preparation and uses 8–9
turmeric and black pepper 8
yellow stain removal 9
turnips
beef stew 86

**V**

vegetables
Buddha bowl 68
five veg tagine 63
turmeric pickles 36

**Y**

yellow rice with coconut halloumi 64
yogurt
turmeric prawn linguine 77